With a Cup of Tea

PAINTINGS BY

Sandy Lynam Clough

HARVEST HOUSE PUBLISHERS
EUGENE, OREGON 97402

Sandy Lynam Clough

What is it about tea that
warms and comforts us so?
That draws us again and
again to enjoy this delightful,
golden beverage? Perhaps it's
the friendship tea inspires.
Or the beautiful ritual
that makes having a cup of tea
special, no matter the occasion.
Whatever the reason, you know
that life is a little richer, a little
smoother, with a cup of tea!

"Come for Tea"

For at least two centuries, "Come for tea"
has been just another way of saying, "Come, let's
share a little bit of our lives together."

EMILIE BARNES

Sandy Lynam Clough

5

6

Sandy Lynam Clough

A joy worth repeating, again and again,
warm conversation, tea, and a friend.

MISS MADELINE

Pleasant words are like honey,
sweet to the soul.

THE BOOK OF PROVERBS

Seldom can the heart be lonely
if it seeks a lonelier still;
Self-forgetting, seeking only
emptier cups of love to fill.

FRANCES HAVERGAL

Sandy Lynam Clough

Now stir the fire,
and close the shutters fast,
Let fall the curtains,
wheel the sofa round;
And while the bubbling
and loud hissing urn
Throws up a steamy column,
and the cups,
That cheer but not inebriate
wait on each,
So let us welcome peaceful
evening in.

WILLIAM COWPER

Tea & Thee

What is there about a cup of tea that invites shared confidences, that nurtures friendship and brings people together? "Tea and sympathy" have been companions for many long years .... Tea fosters friendships by inviting us to be present to one another—right now—in the moment.

EMILIE BARNES

14

Sandy Lynam Clough

Oh, the inexpressible comfort of feeling
safe with a person, having neither to
weigh thoughts, nor measure words—
but pouring them all right out—
just as they are...
DINAH MARIA MULOCK CRAIK

How good is a timely word!
THE BOOK OF PROVERBS

*The daintiness and yet elegance of a
china teacup focuses one to be gentle, to
think warmly and to feel close.*

CAROL & MALCOLM COHEN

Love the Giver

Sandy Lynam Clough

The Ritual of Tea

*The tea ritual feels safe, comforting, inviting.
Quietly and without threat, it calls us out of
ourselves and into relationships. Even the tea
itself—warm and sweet and comforting—
inspires a feeling of relaxation and trust that
fosters shared confidences.*

EMILIE BARNES

Whatever we possess becomes of double value when we have the opportunity of sharing it with others.

BOUILLY

Sandy Lynam Clough

It was George Eliot who earnestly inquired, "Reader, have you ever drunk a cup of tea?" There is something undeniably heartwarming and conversation-making in a cup of steaming hot tea....

It is an ideal prescription for *banishing loneliness. Perhaps it is not so much the tea itself, as the circle of happy friends eager for a pleasant chat.*

BOOK OF ETIQUETTE, 1921

25

A cup of tea in a quiet place
Brings joy to the heart
And a smile to the face.

MISS MADELINE

May you be filled with joy.

THE BOOK OF PSALMS

Give
Thanks

Sandy Lynam Clough

What would the world do without tea?—
how did it exist? I am glad I was not
born before tea.

SYDNEY SMITH

The cup of tea on arrrival at a country house is a thing which, as a rule, I particularly enjoy. I like the crackling logs, the shaded lights, the scent of buttered toast, the general atmosphere of leisured coziness.

P.G. WODEHOUSE

Sandy Lynn Clough

There is a great deal of
poetry and fine sentiment
in a chest of tea.

RALPH WALDO
EMERSON

In The Garden

May the echo of the
teacups' message
be heard not only
on special occasions
but anytime friends
come together.

EMILIE
BARNES